AFRICAN WRITERS SERIES

Founding editor · Chinua Achebe

ANOTHER NIGGER DEAD

poems

TABAN LO LIYONG

HEINEMANN
London · Ibadan · Nairobi

Heinemann Educational Books
48 Charles Street London W1X 8AH
P.M.B. 5205 Ibadan · P.O. BOX 25080 Nairobi
EDINBURGH MELBOURNE TORONTO AUCKLAND
NEW DELHI SINGAPORE HONG KONG KUALA LUMPUR

ISBN 0 435 90116 8

Printed in England by
Cox & Wyman Ltd
London Reading and Fakenham

CONTENTS

bless the african coups
tragedy now means a thing to us

when your child dies tragedy it is
tragedy is that which crushes your best hopes
planted food refuse to grow for tragedys sake
the granary refuses to hold the grains for its sake
foolproof ideas become fools proof for tragedys honour

it is not tragedy
    if your ideas are paltry
it is not tragedy
    if the canvas was so small
it is not tragedy
    if the stakes are minimal
it is not tragedy
    if the risks are not mammoth
it is no tragedy
    if only few common peoples lives are involved
it is no tragedy
    if the bulls escape
it is no tragedy
    if history is not called to compare and judge
it is no tragedy
    if youngsters and figures of speech are not born
it is no tragedy
    if the national ways are not forked

for tragedy involves
    the wringing of hands

[1]

for tragedy involves
    shedding hot tears into your own throat
for tragedy involves
    a sense of doom
for tragedy involves
    small mistakes malignant in the great
for tragedy involves
    some points children could make
for tragedy involves
    not milk but also blood spilt on sand

the tragic is that
    we saw coming like an arrow to a fawn
the tragic is that
    which takes away our major hopes
the tragic is that
    which robs a son of a father before time due
the tragic is that
    which calls for re-examination but without the use for the
                                    experience
the tragic is that
    which charts a counter or un-course
the tragic is that
    which alters a peoples whole concept of good and evil

it is tragedy
    when you curse your god
it is tragedy
    when you question goodness in the world
it is tragedy
    when you are turned into a beast for other men to hunt
it is tragedy
    when overnight you are labelled a sinner

[2]

it is tragedy
    when your friends are out to hang you
it is tragedy
    when your brother betrays you for fun or fund
it is tragedy
    when darkness descends and you know it will suffocate you
it is tragedy
    when doom is all you are left with
it is tragedy
    when your best ideas have no chance for life
it is tragedy
    when you curse and hope it will stick

tragedy is the goats song
    when the butchers knife is near
tragedy is the swans song
    when death is around

can tragedy also be the fire
    which burns the phoenix
can tragedy also be the stage
    in which proteus changes states
can tragedy also be the death
    according to hindu religion
can tragedy also be the death
    of christ on the cross

may tragedy also save us

but tragedy also
    teaches us that we are not the lords of this world
tragedy also
    makes us know our place in this world

tragedy also
   makes man bow down before fate and give to others also
tragedy also
   teaches us final humility
tragedy also
   teaches us the full reality of our confusion
tragedy also
   elevates us to grander levels
tragedy also
   shows us the top of the mountains for the last time
tragedy also
   shines the brightest
tragedy also
   opens the door by mistakes
tragedy also
   ended empires
and tragedy
   is the final point of consciousness from time to time

when the saint sees light
   his joy is equal to the tragic characters last selfawareness
when the discoverer sees his goal
   he has reached the tragedians catching of fire
when the musical composer has brought to life an immortal
                                                        tune
   he has reached the tragedians peak of achievement

for tragedy
   is the writing of a book on the national canvas
tragedy is
   the painting of a sweetbitter picture in dark hues
tragedy is
   the termination of an epic

[4]

it takes more than you and me to become tragic
it requires more than ordinary luck to attain the tragic
it is not just by chance that you reach the mountain top
only a few people are involved in the core of it

weep not child
    human mind has a way out
weep not mother
    other ways shall still be found
weep not man
    all ways lead to salvation
weep not daughters
    we shall overcome
weep not schoolboys
    take up the load where we left it

indomitable farmers
    cultivate another garden
for man must eat
    if you cant drink milk
    cant orange fruits do

hidden from the comedians eyes are the secrets of the tragic
the cynic can never perceive of that which is tragic
a born optimist will never realize when the cloud is overcast
a child who does not know the full effects of fire will never
        take precautions
a wanderer without a boundary will never know where
        tragedy begins and where it ends
those who do not fear death are outside the perimetre of the
        doomed

[5]

those who have no thought of immortality are blind to the
      dictates of the tragic
a man who cant store food for tomorrow will never feel the
      pangs of the tragic beast

for without hope
   tragedy has never an existence
without adherence
   tragedy never dwells amongst us
the tragic sense of life
   scares away the boys from the men
for the human mind yearns for greatness
   even if man perishes on the way
looking at the stars is no tragedy
   but maintaining there is heaven leads us there
seeing that the world is round is one thing
   but tell the priest that thats your view and tragedybound
      you are
for tragedy also grows extending its boundary with increase
      of knowledge
for the many readers of existentialism tragedy is merely a
      ghost
and those who have seen the theatre of cruelty do not know
      the difference between the play and the real
and people who dwell in the ideas of the absurd are well
      indoctrinated against shedding tears as aristotle would
      want us to
and biochemicophysicists will never know what tragedy is
      except in another gear
therefore tragedy exists
and does not exist
i know some who maintain it does not exist
and others who swear tragedy is right at home

[6]

those who truck in feelings use tragedy as the touchstone of
     greatness and petty blindness
those whose feelings are anaesthetized do not feel the change
     of weather

objectively speaking tragedy is a child of our baser and primal
     instinct and impetuosity to evolution
those emancipated from feelings see transgressors of natural
     laws falling and remark
     ANOTHER NIGGER DEAD

the filed man laughed and said
    nationalization is the answer
a reporter jested
    what is the question
the filed man laughed and said
    neocolonialism is the problem
and a boy asked
    whence comes neocolonialism
the filed man laughed and said
    from the west of course
and a cynic said
    we are lucky for weve no neocolonialists
the filed man laughed and said
    you are right how wonderful
but the cynic declared
    westerners from the east are friends in deed
the filed man laughed and said
    from the east friendship only flows

the filed man laughed again and said
    nationalize all industries for they came from the west
a functionary reported done
the filed man laughed again and said
    nationalize all banks for they come from the west
a functionary reported done
the filed man laughed again and said
    nationalize all houses for they come from the west
a functionary reported done
the filed man laughed again and said
    nationalize all thoughts for they are produced by the west

a functionary reported done
the filed man laughed again and said
   nationalize everything for possessions come from the west
a functionary reported done
the filed man laughed again and said
   nationalize even that which has not been nationalized for it
                         also comes from the west
a functionary reported
   we have at last nationalized POVERTY

then the filed man laughed the last laugh and said
   didnt i tell you my people
   with good advice from the east
   we can triumph over all our difficulties
   when you follow your leaders
   nothing will go wrong
   our present success shows what can be achieved
   with a little effort
   with the right leadership
   the one leadership

to miss li
the way to create excellence is one
socialism racism capitalism communism fascism newism
distinction is sought with tears and blood
the yardstick should flog to death
the deranged should cry and ask for more
the pill the idiots love should be by the door
each head becomes a regulator firm and strong
and outside noise is faint like echoes from mars
the moment of translation is the arrival supreme
the rubicons macbeth traversed
two minutes should do the works of ages gone
the football is kicked the foot hurts but the ground is grazed
from the rock massive a chrysalis entrances as clear as day
the wallowers in the darkness of mediocrity gape and gaze
hence excellence will always be my song
thus keeping us in shape

there goes my son
a bright lad doing well at school
my heart flows with honey when people remark
hell be as successful as his daddy
others will say
his father was the best hunter with spears
but his pen signs fat cheques
others will envy
brought up well at home
doing well at school
yet others will envy
prosperity down in the farms with conditions changed
is prosperity achieved after school
yet there will be those
a hard worker is a hard worker
here or there
thats the selection which changes not
hence my sons an elect

with purity hath nothing been won
greece came not thru purity
christ died through the impure
only with impurity hath japan moved ahead
the american beast came about through things impure
purity kills creativity in the womb
impurity spreads with health
eve ate the apple for impuritys sake
my heart bless thyself
thou truckest not with things that are pure
impurity fills you up like angels of god
thou art greater than earth and hell
for impurity limiteth the child in the cradle
impurity is boundless like my soul

blood iron and trumpets
blood iron and trumpets
forward we march
(others fall on the way)
blood iron and trumpets
blood iron and trumpets
we shall hack to kill and cure
blood iron and trumpets
singers of the datsun blue
forward we drive breaking the records
blood iron and trumpets
let bullets find their targets and the earth be softened
blood iron and trumpets
let the dogs of war rejoice
and the carrion birds feed
we are reducing population sexplosion
blood iron and trumpets
the uniformed machines are around
put on your helmet iron and the rest
blood iron and trumpets
only thru fire can we be baptized to mean business
so once again
blood iron and trumpets
we shall always march along
blood iron and trumpets
blood iron and trumpets
blood alone

i was weaned from my playmates right in the womb
and grew up at the age of two never passing through
    playtime stage
have never known how to play a game and those who have
    tried found me without mirth
hence the rules for a mock are quite apart from my own
    constitution

i was raised amongst people who were strangers to us
and learnt their acts at the time i was learning ours
had no time for games since the doubleload of learning was
    quite engrossing
hence ive no regret to state that i cant fit into a team game

born a misfit by constitution since morbidity rules my acts
and loved my thoughts which i stripped in solitude without
    another body around
thoughts beyond adults who had their childhood with them
    unto age grey with hair
hence i kept aloof from others and cherished the thoughts
    engraved in books

learning life from books is my first nature now

me alone am company enough

when i am down and low
   some clever or dessicated wise man talks to me in tongues
when i am happy or sad
   i set my thoughts on paper for amusing myself

when am glad i celebrate with others their joys in life
hence am company enough
when am glad i celebrate with others their joys in life
hence am company enough

i have seen people exciting themselves replacing hercules
i have seen the rock come crushing down
i have seen fame crumpled under the publics feet
i have seen hero erased and villain engraved
and friends revealed the enemies

what friendship do i further seek more constant than i

what boils in a mans blood so that he dares the hornets in
        order to run to my house
are some people prone to running so that tranquility bites
        them like the snake and they needs must hop and howl
i cant understand why some peoples children have no
        homoestasis in their bodily constitutions to keep an
        even keel
i cant see why some cars do not develop suspensors to keep
        them gliding at the same horizon instead of going up
        and down

for beware the voice of the air that is hot
guard particularly against the upright sun
forget not to shelter from thunder without any rains
when dogs mate with cat offer usual blessings
hysterias portend to national calamities

    beware of the fatal reptiles
when villagers take laws into their hands your testes have
        shrunk

unmarried women should not marry wives by proxy
for their children are a curse to the unblemished sheep
widows particularly should not walk with shrunken or
       flabbied breasts bare
before your mother opens her thing to curse you run to the
       hilltop
when your father is bathing take to your heels
beggars who are also informers deserve a kick
if every year is not a teacher check the kilo meat
for why do grass and flowers and chameleons grow
i tell you the age of innocence is passed
and women copulate through their mouths

   death
   where is thy sting

why is eating so good and the eaters blind
why is joy so fair and the carousers deaf
why is eating so good and the eaters so blind
why is greed such an attraction and the inflicted insatiate
and why is calamity so black and heavy people cry out and
       need a pull
why is ignorance so massive we are always asking for help

i brought doubt into the world
the world doubted me instead
such is fate
master confuser

dancing ripples so dazzling
epitaphs unchained to a pole
twilight phantoms grounded a dream
underfoot sun on my head

lets go back to land
and leave city to whom
gyrations amidst a lumpen wool
avuncular beckoning
dear mary whetting

eighteen summers had passed
i bagged my first benz
retarded growths my lot
another tenant to be

born in hunger
hungry for children
unquenched with dowry
hes my rival
father-in-law

ho that odysseus is here
telemachus doing own thing
white ants desecrate umbis cord
blazers of foreign ways
rootland smothered in darkness

blazers of foreign ways
telemachus intending forgery
odysseus off again
white ants tramp umbis cord
rootland sunk in darkness

chicken scratching surface memory
moles boring tunnels to blind depths
ignorance and fear protect us
sink skeleton please waterbuck

too clever by half
halfwit fooled with fashions
human beings went to prison
claimed he was a writer

let me suck your ulcers lazarus
the pestilences in our heart
salvation to be gained
by fathoming

the fast foot defeats itself
oedipus your fathers dead
anges foot is sick
slow-witted prometheus

scum thinning in pails
sperm of god smothering sea
served vitality
absent agent
we lack no fire nor water

other lives
scapegoats of burdens
worship the masks

hot suns up again
scorched testes to distill
more funnels than ever

european colonizers mastered our men so well
it proved difficult to shake them off our backs
only we sperm fertilizers

freelance critics circumscribe perimetres
consign to gehenna and posterity
what an elusive age
no homer
prize distributed

cynicism
in my hour of pride i courted you
humility
let me rest my future in thee

ecstasy
eternal feel of lemon leaf
the depth of darkness
its obscurity
how monumental
a mine of bricks
groping in the womb

leopard dyed himself browner
to show hes a lion
headcount reports
noahs wrong

the cloud reshaped a hippo
i hailed the rubber given
when the butterfly came
i felt my bladder bursting

the multicoloured people are red
with their mouths in the back
their husbands bear children
so constantly clad

the african coup is an old beast
insecure under rug
youngsters with short memory
wheres the future

sympathisers with the cheated
vulgar is the taste
standard bearers of fate
hooting owls in darkness

amoebas shed no tears
theirs not to think
theres more to life than brain and thought
wildflowers die unnoticed

campus points fixed in void
cocks run from eagles
the lure of maelstrom
i fear no death

[24]

urgen clad in iron
green grass across
bright moon enticing
serenade

the rind
mother to seed
the juice
mere appetizer

obstinate lover is
sceptical
requite my love

my selfishness is boundless
immersed in the self am i day and night
grant me the hidden thread
loving god

denied the lives of cats
let the many grow through me
am only a weak vessel
cant stand a split

i wished and found my tentative selves
the coats never fitted well
return to the self
and be

[26]

the many make the me to dance
keep my fixity oh lord
and limit my visits

let my answer to the pull of the powerful other be
the sufficiency of the one
the glory of the many

that restlessness within my heart
the samples of water and salt
the stillness deeper than depth
bar external strivings

shouting to raise my voice
only whispered and passed unnoticed
this tin
not even an ore

withstanding the gale is hard enough
grant thy slave a breathing space
to behold his thigh in a flesh

i swelled my head with thy bounties
teach me to bank aright
you who never grudged me transgressions

[28]

my inner eye now sees
too much light it sees
my ear has no room
to hear in depth and long

sensuousness is my bane
i ride on the crest
drown me oh lord
bear me anew

because i have grey hair
why assume acts of ages
wisdom of youth should mellow
in mind or time

[29]

i lived in my future
and exhausted my stock
and lost my youth
grow up
theyd said
and left me killed

i shall now stand still
and withstand external growth
and round up my sphere
however small its mine

striving for effects
mocked by results
treacherous shortcuts
have joy in the attempts
talent bore interest
shanti shanti shanti

[30]

fix your gaze on higher things
eunuch
the wellworn path is large
plunge yourself into the needles eye
bruises that last

take your gift lord if i am writing to be a writer
but open my soul to understand my restlessness

i speak the word to know it tomorrow
a babbler by the seaside
the word is the world
    world   word

what unspeakable guilt hides in my heart
my stomach is so fat
my navel cant be seen
chameleon cling to my tail

washing ones brains needs bleaches
the hardgrained were superforged
pride has no deterrent
how hard is rebirth

be a fool with your sins
card your intestines in the market
let them laugh who are crying
pathless explorers

holier than thou
my sin supreme
a few depths away
humbleness to steer my ship
sorry for this compensation
forgive

i sleep with my eyes open
intent on arresting dream
thus i dont dance
yet demand the laurel

the secret of fools eludes me
the prostitute bore jesus
i saw the yellow eye of the sun
still wrapped in darkness

i love man so much
i present to him
fruits of my selfishness
payment inexhaustible
virtue of public appearance

how wide a vocabulary must a man have
to explore meanings in the world
sometimes words fail me

with a bounty of words
the love of toys increaseth
the common labourer subsists
but struggles to feed

the grids are well set
the woofs are all in line
shuttle then back and forth
explore the hidden lines and nooses

if i appear foolish in the eyes of others
what if i am truly a fool
shouldnt i glorify
in my folly

his highness the masquerader
lives the role he plays
and takes a holiday
i wonder

[35]

the phoenix is an idiot
living to die to live
drosophila populate the earth
yet theyre not fabulous

the growth of a poet is the growth of a seer
from the rocks to purify the ore
nugget gold

building a life philosophy
through juggling with words
fashioning home truths
by exploring the obscure

coarseness bespeaks a journey unbegun
the unshifted blocking the sieve
clarity without clouds
darkness impervious

through the superficial
learn the hidden meanings
the map of eternity
glitters in a glance

the growth of selfawareness
has caught me like a fever
i pray for birth
but whats the name

[37]

i review my life through the line ive written
and pass judgement on the world around me
clean the sentence

evolution never helped amoeba fashion feet
through trials and errors the tortoise learnt a lesson
you create yourself

through involvement and immersion
ive widened my meanings of words
the removal of a cataract
(or) the illumination of the general scene

[38]

im not yet of age
trusting in others pathways
are they my failures
or me their failures?

freedom nags at my soul
the late development of a younger son
the impertinence of a toothless boy

the inadequacy of the human lamp
the impenetrability of the dense fog
the boundlessness of the world of search

[39]

to give up and curse god
is to despair too soon
even the blind struggle to see
have courage ablebodied

not for another world is my search
my oldest bride is too new
increase the sum of our appraisal

with all my clarity if im understood
the more reason to persist
local underdevelopment
efforts and concentrated aid

[40]

virginity is the result of ignorance
barren fruit of caution and timidity
purity is achieved through cleansing
selfwilled act

when the horse has lost appetite to move
rider dont force a mechanical move
nothing so pathetic
compulsion against inertia

the chosen tongue is lost
should acquire another in time
meanwhile remain speechless
bear with me

it is not a sin to envy another
jealousy is tinged with ideas murderous
the envious can stir towards challenges
(count me one oh lord)

why do indians meditate deeper than i
my lamp please give me light
is poverty a source of wealth

let me not trifle with matters of life and death
if my mission is true let me not be misled

doubt stirs my heart like the gale of eve
are my ideas shallow and my words pendulous

melodramatic is the pit i detest
at least give me a comic relief

hiding behind skirts of others
i hide beneath the shades
sunlight almost blinded me

[43]

i dont drink with harry
call me no misanthrope
father saw my loneliness
and gave me brothers to keep

not pride but glorification of my maker
makes me use my talents for what they are worth
ive clowned enough

courtesies are also curtseys
but they demand practice to perfect
only fools write poems by chance

[44]

intelligence tests set by mafia
will baffle you and i
except you travel together

is it to be born today
and never speak a word from the cave
without landing even on the moon

i know what it means to fall in love with words
they are so inadequate
and my stock runs dry

[45]

with gadgets you explore neurons and stars
to use the eye to see the mind
is world within words

how to tempt heaven with words
without serving ones full term
is miscarriage without the rights

in a material age
live a life spiritual
thereby supplying the necessary tension
and the missing pillar

[46]

id have loved god more
had christian missionaries confirmed my superstitions
its hard to believe
after being undeceived

when i begin cutting throats
i have maintained goodwill long enough
i can kill with clean conscience

the seasonal flooding
deposited their sediments
and killed the oyster

[47]

love others to exploit them
make yourself whole like a peacock

were i the lousy lover
id not dream of killing
for my passion is at its pitch

he walks a pillar
with allotted few mistakes
hid in briefcase
woe is me
discovering mistakes daily

[48]

how grateful he is
buying bonuses for begging
another time

through generosity
we squander our goods to buy love
but the daily due increaseth

to love one
is to hate all else
how small is the human organ

[49]

call your sins virtues
have a long life
(so) steer clear of rocks
travel light
carrying a conversion table

lying proves more explanations
projections of facts
real satellites

ideas are strange beasts
worshippers by beholders unto death
dole out in standard metric measures

when i die let my lovers live
except the suicide prone

i love life so
i dont want to die
unknown
unremembered

inadequacy fills us like a void
to be filled and propped by work
and achievements and notoriety

selfprotection is oldage
wisdom insulates so well
presence when absence was needed

all men seek happiness
in very unlikely places

look at the jealous and malicious
inducing hell into the hall of pleasure
humans clad a la devils

[52]

nothing good but mediocrity
thus we cut our thoughts
and excellence rides unbridled

a conscience flower grows in my backyard
who will pluck it to beautify his room

go forth you dove or hawk
spring child of my head

born between then and now
hippies we all became
wearing strange suits
and being naked

[53]

i walked among men in america for a year without a human
soul to solace me

my spring came one summer when a homegirl left albions
shore for a hunt in the lands that are new

i married a girl who did not know me but i was educated and
in a university

me i married a girl i did not know but thought she was
educated enough to be sensible

my inlaws know the value of education for i married from the
university house

it was a house of plenty for my fatherinlaw got the highest
dowry from me in all acholiland

i married into a house of respectability for everybody there
puts up a false public image

like an educated man i respected my wife and she did things
her own way

i even agreed to a joint savings account to be a security for
my two growing sons

i bought a family car for taking the children and me to
school with my wife keeping it all day long

one day i returned from a conference in indiana only to find
the joint account cleared and closed

i said lets discuss finance for i want to build a house for us
and our children but my wife said no

one wednesday afternoon we came home to find my wifes
new vw parked in my compound so thats where my
money had gone

i said ah taban someone is playing with your testicles to find
   out if you are a eunuch or a man

me with my village mentality i said sister lets talk this over
   with broinlaw
and bro when he came was all fire with guns and shooting
   wild
me when i saw red death staring me in the face i said taban
   where is your sense of survival put a great distance
   between yourself and this monster here
when i returned i found my house ready for the next occupant
sister and brother had hauled away all the possessions my
   dead father had left me and those i had acquired with
   the sweat of my brow
it was great fun also for them to kidnap my two sons my
   fathers grandsons and take them to their house the
   way some people have enriched themselves at my
   expense

me in my oldfashioned way i said sister lets consult daddyinlaw
   in his maturity some wisdom must come
but daddyinlaw looks me over calls me a gorilla and wonders
   which bush i was ever gathered from
me still in my naivete i said sister lets try mummyinlaw she
   should remember the pangs of birth and childbearing
   im sure shed encourage a staytogether
but foolishly i narrated to her her daughters escapades while
   she lived with me six years and motherinlaw being
   the source of all the quiet and peace in my house
   politely informed the world and whoever cared to
   know that the lady before us is her examplar daughter
   and that was that

in my slowwittedness i said taban for once stop and think for
six years you have gone forward married forgiven
suffered and hoped something isnt amiss

then the fog cleared a little just a little to open my eyes to
the fact that in this wide world some big homes rise
out of lawlessness

and who was this gorilla to come at the eleventh hour to
begin instituting a system of respectability patience
consideration foresight and humility

that which grew out of opportunism bullyism brutality
flourishes by the integral laws of grabiousness and
burns up within the third generation without one to
inherit it

in my humble way i thought it was for these emergencies
that society decreed for exogamous marriages so that
new vitalities get instilled into families but i understand
this is a voice from my valley

crestfallen i walk away from my inlaws with my eldest sister
the sole witness of my own humiliation she the
standin for my father who had traversed this distance
so many times to acquire for me a wife that wife with
himself falling dead by the wayside in utter exhaustion

one day in my foolishness i applied for a job in my propertied
and highpowered brotherinlaws university and to
doubly display my dunderheadedness sent him word
that i wanted to storm his solid fortress with a force
sixteen pages strong plus three auxilliaries

i duly reminded him to keep his promise to me earlier on that
in the event of my catching a fancy for their house of
fashions i should keep him posted as he hobnobs
with the big man who keeps the gate and surely a

word from his own mouth would perform the magic
of opening the door to obscure people like myself
who would soon bloom aided by the strong light
my 'brother' looks at me and says help me god forever
deliver mine enemies into mine hands this taban
broadcasts his manhood abroad accuses me of cowing
under my sisters thumb where does he think i get the
manhood to do all the things i have done if not from
this tightly knit family he abuses we shall see
sure enough the day of reckoning comes along and 'bro'
breakfasted on venom goes to the committee of
guillotine lifts up from obscurity three people to
profess their ignorance and shoves taban right into
the tartarian depth where hes expected to learn some
manners and his alphabet of who is who

me i said to myself taban cool it baby cool it you have reached
this far by hope perseverence hardwork and solid
personal achievement continue to engrave your name
on barks of trees and some day somebody who loves
qualities will lift you up and if wild grass blocks the
path to your trees even in future without your seeing
some people will ask after you but produce more
solid works
the fashionmakers get instant fame which gets changed before
the year is over these famous businessmen also go to
the latrine like you but they care so much about
gratifying their tastebuds they are also biting at
something beware of joining in a game you are not
fitted for the instant people cant live till tomorrow
you are halfalive today halfalive tomorrow and
halfalive the day after isnt that reward enough thus i
nursed myself and soothed my wounds

i am learning let me succeed i am learning let me increase in
understanding society and men out of love and hatred
create heroes and sentence to perdition overnight it
requires unearthly qualities for the blackbooked to
continue their undigested lumps of gall without
committing murder

i open my eyes and see houses which look as if they will ever
remain on the hilltop
but i open my eyes and see some men act as if they have four
testicles like the squirrel
but i open my eyes and see some women who live on their
family names but are doing their best to dirten their
own

i did not choose to be born poor my father had consideration
for other fellow human beings so we were rich in
hospitality without people understanding the real
nature of my endowment and debits they are kicking
me from one side of the road to the other

what am i supposed to do shed tears day and night and curse
myself no even if i live poor and obscure i know
human beings live by consideration respect and
humility hence i curse those who degrade such human
qualities and sentiments

i declare only grandsons and daughters of my 'father' inlaw
who practise humility will amount to something all
the others will wither and burn like chaff and i
include my two sons in this prophesy or curse

when some people dig with hoes and others with tractors
who reaps the seeds of justice and truth and honour and the
      chaff
for it quite perplexes me my people please help me
when some people fly in aeroplanes and others walk on
      foot
who are the repositories of wisdom and commonsense
my people please help for the wise is not the constitutionally
      dull not the saturninely opportunistic

i am afraid there are new seeds we still misname and old ones
      we dont name and we are sorely grieved to eat fruits
      without names
for how shall i explain my death my people
what shall i call the ailment that has killed me please help
      explain
am i dead in nomans land
where shall i be buried when i die in the land nobody is
      allowed to shed tears in
perhaps i should have been born a brother to my grandfather
then i would have honoured him and he me with warm
      embraces
and in the book of good deeds my grand total would have
      been solid substantial
or perhaps i should have been born in russia a brother of
      stalin
then i would have dyed myself red and with achievements
bloody won a niche for myself in the hall of fame
or perhaps i am to be reborn in the generation to come

here i am communicating with my friend the faithful paper
in confidence
due to hesitancy among those with ears and the lack of
vocabulary among the eager but uncoached
for in times of drought nobody shares water with his
neighbour
and when all the sheep are dressed as wolves it is difficult to
single out the real from the fake
hence i am not surprised others are using me and not
confiding
for the tower has been rebuilt and collapsed
and there is a scattering as of dry seeds in a strong wind
and i am still sitting on my log of old
and the young seeds and light flit by some resting on my
laps a while
it is true i should not brush them away
but it is also true they should have fallen on the ground
the gehenna role does not hold sway over me anymore
i am nobodys hero but dead peoples
leave my grave alone for its oracles confirm your hopes and
fears

the man who entrusts his fame into the hands of the people is
holding an egg that is already broken
artists are fortunate for they are their own makers
and herders of goats and sheep are unmade through the
traitors they breed
i am writing because i cant herd and theres no substitute
around
i have been asked to loan my services to a cause i dont know
and my questions plain and short were these
why is eating so good and the eaters blind
why is joy so fair and the carousers deaf

why is greed such an attraction and the inflicted so insatiate
and why is calamity so black and heavy people cry out and
        would be pulled
and why is ignorance so universal there will always be people
        asking for help

since it gives me no joy to save alcoholics
since i add nothing to vary my stature by associating with
        the addicted
since i hope for no reward by doing good
my bough is not a nest for sinners
please leave me alone
me and my tranquillity
melancholy and me are friends
your presence lightens not a bit my load
it is your sport to sign your name in running water
mine is to stay put
do your thing and i will do my own
i rejoice in my existence afterall it is all ive got
learn to praise your own but dont make it a burden for others
        to carry
mine is heavy enough i cant even stand up
anyway

heres something ive always wanted to talk about

the marriage between negritude and debased whitetude a man lived in a hut with mudded wattle for a wall the earth for a floor and grass for a roof top on branches of trees because he couldnt live in something else

his hut is part and parcel of his life its cycle its entity and its culture so he builds the hut as the thing to do for it has been done for years and years place of habitation he sees in a hut born there grown up there eaten there fucked there and possibly died there it is house home everything and as it should be

now another man comes around and laughs long and bitter then he stops and begins to wonder whether he should not have a change in his own home and he decides that of course there should be a change and he is going to adopt the outside tramellings of what the nigger is doing and so he comes around to the nigger and says he says hey man how would you like me to join you for a change for you know what im so tired and fed up of life in them storey houses now i wana come down to nature and fuck like you do right here on this earth floor and ill get my broad and lay her right here as the good lord had wanted us to and you can go ahead and lay your own miss right here beside me so that my woman and i can keep to your rhythm and we can also smoke maryjane right here equality has arrived and theres no difference between you and me for am i not your brother right on the floor and so the game is initiated and the nigger whose hair has now grown larger than a lions says yea man and and and he says soul brother you are wonderful and please go ahead and fuck right here on my floor and damn them civilized people

BATSIARY IN SANIGRALAND

In the year 3.5 c.m. Nabat akhen-a-Ghose will have completed his long-awaited research into the analytical, descriptive, and predictive natures of the Fauna and Flora (perhaps 'batsiary' as other independent and rival bird-watchers using a different system of nomenclature would have us informed) which have existed, still exist, and will probably exist in Sanigraland, an island bounded both by sunset and sunrise.

The diasporic, historical and behavioural natures of the same species in the macro-micros have already received enough attention from the Anglo-German Muller and his descendants, which include such personalities like Myrdal, de Toqueville (both working exhaustibly in Antland – the land of ant-hills and ant-rush from nowhere to nowhere); external soul mapping has vied with internal self-search in the huge inguanaland, although where calypso sings the approach from within is more illuminative than the external facades erected by ill- and well-wishers.

It is therefore our fervent wish that Nabat akhen-a-Ghose will oblige us with the Heartlandic map, with many super imposed colour slides to bring out in bold-relief and yet capture the kaleidoscopic permutations and transfigurations he would like us to observe on his new coat-of-arms.

Museums are the shrines of muses. Despite Freud's protestations, isn't it conceivable etymologically that muses and moses are related? If they are, then both are the products of the Nile, monumental, formed and half-formed, and fittingly described by the adventurous Antony in these revealing sentences.

... They take the flow o' the Nile
By certain scales i' the pyramid; they know
By the height, the lowness, or the mean, if dearth
Or foison follow. The higher Nilus swells
The more it promises; as it ebbs, the seedsman
Upon the slime and ooze scatters his grain,
And shortly comes to harvest.

To that mosaic, let's add Lepidus's observations about the strange serpents of ancient Egypt: 'Your serpent of Egypt is bred now of your mud by the operation of your sun; so is your crocodile'. And to cap it all, the difficult nature of the enigma akhen-a-Ghose is grappling with symbolically threw Antony to the ground. Here's his death-cry when defeated in divining the manner of the Nile crocodile:

It is shaped, sir, like itself, and it is as broad as it hath breadth; it is just so high as it is, and moves with its own organs; it lives by that which nourisheth it; and the elements once out of it, it transmigrates.

Perhaps the children of sphinxes can give us more meaningful insights into the natures of their forebears?
The Nile valley was the bottom lode-centre of the world. And akhen-a-Ghose discovered, through the painstaking employment of Jung's instrument called 'collective unconscious' allied to the 'archetype', that when the water-mass fed by the Nile was millions of years later named the Middle-Earth-Sea, the dwellers on its shores, through a secret thread renamed a truth. The loadstar, spun by the hand of the master cricketer, swung first to Algeria, and later hid in the southern cold-lands, snuffing out of place the warm tropics which had had for years optimistically basked there.

Movement was our watchword in the above paragraph. Now, to the new coat-of-arms Nabat will be designing.

Liver-shaped we are sure it will be: liver-shaped but spread-eagled. The central part will spread to the source of the Nile. Wings will flap east-west. The mane and head-feathers will point upwards but appear arrested in the manner of a hawk whose head has hit a cold electric wire. The whole contraption will look like a nailed mendicant whose heart still pulsates. And the creatures spawning on the Nile bank, past and present should be seen, or dug-up-to-be seen a la Leakey crawling and going which-ever-way.

With the stage already set, let's divine the crawlings of these water-or-blood-gorged creatures. They can be seen disgorging their contents and leaving their permanent and impermanent marks on the whole liver-shape. But again, some of these, like the pythons seem bulky in parts and stationary while digesting a kill. Others again, like the locust are engaged both in chewing long grass-leaves with their anteriors while their posteriors are excreting the interminable thing through its passage in the alimentary canal. Again others, like the crocodile, have their mouths wide open while awaiting the accumulation of flies. Dogs were not yet catalogued then. But if they were, we are sure some would have been found sound asleep.

Now, in order to re-understand Jung, let's appraise you with a future chapter from akhen-a-Ghose's thesis. Chapter XIVX, hairs two thousand from the left brow, disserts on the nature of cactuses. (It also reveals Zeno to us as well as fulfilling his mission.)

Live lives in the atmosphere like chemicals.
It is inhaled into the child and given out at death.
A man is a walking chemical bubble

Tied down by blood, bones, and flesh: other chemicals all
Man himself is one: a cactus tree.
Its branches are strewn all over where they behaved
   chamelon,
The amoeba breaks with life in fractions.
A piece of magnet is polarized.
Manandwomanandotheranimalsandthings broke off a
   tree;
The tree broke off humid ground.
What we call knowledge is a chemical substance.

– And he goes on to say that the world, including space is one
solid continuum. Achilles can't catch the tortoise because he
won't be able to move since one ice cube cannot leave its
station. And also that an arrow cannot be shot because it is
already encased in a diamond-case.

That being the case, the science of archememory was born
and accepted by the universities of Oxford, Leningrad, and
Harvard; Padua, Montevideo, and Nairobi. But, such a
science is not new, after all. What we have had are successful
take-overs. This science dethroned psychology, which had
already couped against philosophy, which had taken-over
from religion, which was a natural successor to superstition,
which is still with us.

Regard this simple principle: if you have a hard stump on
your bottom, doesn't it broadcast the fact that your tail is
recessional? And didn't Eliot sing: 'In my beginning is my
end'? Or is it vice versa?

But, are all those satellites shot into the firmament going to
return to earth? Or will they revolve round the moon like
Verne's dog? Now, what about Armstrong's footsteps on the
moon? I have sneaky feeling that some platforms, like trolls,

support their own lives, and in themselves are sufficient, and know not Caesar.

But, like any evidence against his theory or not, Nabat akhen-a-Ghose was also a veritable cataloguer. He took note of a phenomenon called Leakey's-search-for-his-tail. And this led him to note, with unease, an anachronistic species called 'extinct-moderns'. (But, this also justifies Jung.)

Nobody really knows in what year c.m. drosophilas have been here with us on earth. But most entomological experts, scientific experts, biology experts, zoology experts are agreed that drosophilas will incontestably inherit the earth. But we must distinguish their mode of operation from the chameleon's. For, whereas chameleons survive through camouflage, adjusting their chlorophylls according to the hues of the locale, drosophilas are a virulent lot, arduous and full-believers in their capacities to reproduce, and cactus-like, live even without the Nile moisture. Taking order from nobody, and respecting neither rank, nor size, nor birth, drosophilas assert themselves against all odds. They are sure that when the chips are down, they will be on top. In any case, you cannot annihilate them without bringing about your demise also. There are they who are cancerous and din our ears with each cock-crow and at sunset. Now that they glut Antland and are itchy on Maneland do they have a room for manoeuvre in Heartland? The answer to that question is fore-knowledge.

'Circumspectively, the chameleon has arrived, at last,' said the lame dog to the blind mole. But haven't we seen chameleons in the morning looking like antique objects, and now when the millimetre is up, nodding their heads like driedden the brother of lizards admitting that Uncle Pig is right, after all? There is something called a fixed gut and a coatable exterior recladdable at each turn of weather or terrain. Can we expect a veritable journey to the interior from the chameleons? Hardly, except if they be x-rayed. And again, they can't usurp the tortoise's role.

'It flieth by night and feedeth on air,' so goes Sir Thomas Browne's entry on the batsiary in his book called *Pseudodoxia Academica*. He continued: 'It hath the heirs of a mouse, the armes of a duck-foot, but twittereth like a bird.' And in his review of the said work, akhen-a-Ghose quotes Sanigraland's seniorest citizen, none other than Zinjanthropus. The entry goes: 'Zinjanthropus thoughted there existing within a batsiary a batling within a batlette, within a batsen within a batson within a bate . . . more in the nature of aliquot part of aliquot part of a given number.' And Nabat akhen-a-Ghose was provoked enough to see for himself the generations within Banquo's itinerant ghost. Catching or is it 'caughting'? the biggest and lookingly most pregnant batsiary, akhen-a-Ghose dissected the veritable creature to his chagrin. His conclusion: 'Mythological batsiaries need not be looked at with the naked eye. You see them like your father, with your mind's eye'. (However, I feel compelled to footnote the above entry. Batsiaries might have changed their natures since the renowned scholar wrote those words. For, in our own time have we not seen a batling within a batsiary? Readers, reflect). So, chameleons, to begin off with are colourless but possibility – pregnant. Should the environment change green, greenness catches them like the fleuva on the Nile. If the sun-rise is red, red banners they hoist up but, always ready to replace these with the acceptable hues. And, if the midlands are black-and-white then their coats are black-and-white like football uniforms. 'But, I must warn you,' quoth akhen-a-Ghose, 'they are a most difficult lot to identify, as on no occasion did I speak to them adopting different poses without hearing an echo of my voice in their words.'

A trial chapter begins: 'Albionman is born stigmatized'. Somewhere down the page, full of doodlings, I detected a feeble attempt at clarification, with the lone words 'white of species'. But on the next page, written possibly after a long sleep, or with the stimulation of music, if not sex, if not scent, we get this bold entry: 'They stink like skunks if you don't like them. But are easy to deal with since their infirmities are unmaskable and therefore pose no big problems for those who have definite ends and calculated tactics. For, these are they who changeth not but are afraid of the sun.' Continues the page: 'In their fixed natures they resemble the armadillos whose contents are fixed, whose capacities change not, and who would rather harden their backs against the whips of learning than become something else'. (It is day-clear that an Albionman will never become a drosophila. For, their birth-constitution regulates their forward life. Like the UN speaker said, 'If the members on my two hands can't hear, and those in my past can't hear either, then Mr. Chairman, you should hear me very well since you are sitting in my future.'

But, why should armadillos eat ants? I am sure (and Nabat should also agree with me since I am his editor and, therefore, am strategically placed to control his destiny) that it is because ants give armadillos the most challenge. If it were not so, why should ants – small things that they are – see fit to defend their nests and hills against big marauders of the armadillo's stature? You realize that worker-bees are also ants and they sting 'in defence of the nest'. Then there are the askari-ants who guard the bridge-path against infidels, thieves, witches; child stealers, rapers, lootists; double-mouth snakes, ulterior-motivers and materialists, when an old homestead is being repaired or a new one is being set-up. And, although some of them kill snakes to the accompaniment of music, they invariably mean business in silence with their small darts like Lilliputians. I do not think ants will grow in size although they may use more concentrated, and therefore more lethal, poisoned arrows. 'These are they,' let's consult the script, 'who guard our shrines, kill (if not pester – or is it 'fester'?) our internal and external enemies. They sit on my right. And, one of them recently, like the Nile royalties, or the Maneland spy, willfully effected his own demise in the land of the Big smoke and sun. Duty-conscious they are.' ('Robot-men, these. Allied with tradition or market owner'. *Editor*.)

Need we talk of puppies and not invoke fresh memories of tooth-less bulldogs? Or is John Bull constitutionally different from the mongrels? But, Pavlov had remarked somewhere that 'they bark most when afraid most' (*John Smith's translation*). I am sure he, (Pavlov) meant old toothless bull-dogs. For, young puppies bark, we surmise because they haven't yet grown teeth or learnt to bite. 'There is hope in them,' continues akhen-a-Ghose, 'although they spend more energy exercising their lungs than their jaws'.

(On two separate occasions I have found Nabat akhen-a-Ghose exposing himself. Why should he, talking about ants say: 'They sit on my right'? And in the above passage why that 'there is hope in them'? But the last remark cannot pass uncriticized. (I suppose editors are allowed that constructive role.) For, do we really know whom, what, or where these puppies will bite when they come of age? And like the pupas they are, what creatures will they hatch into? For the time being let's resolve the contradictions by quoting Catman-Mao: 'Let a thousand puppies grow'. Although here again, surely nobody will take away from them their rights to growl? Or what?)

Cats, as we understand, feed on rats. But rats as the blackman said live in primarily two different locations: town and country. The country ones are they who are bred in the country (a tautology, accepted, but, so what?), being relatively old, speaking an ancient tongue (archeologically speaking in both the Youngian and Leakian sense) 'with volubility' they come to the arena as they are, teaching lessons on tree-climbing (as if the land is still full of buffaloes) and circumsuspectly unstirred by the cracklings of smoke-sticks. It is not doubted that buffaloes still exist, and my mentor akhen-a-Ghose himself intends to include that fact in his final volume when it gets written 1.5 c.m. since. But, what is being pointed out is that smoke-sticks exist as well, and are increasing in algebraic progression while buffaloes are decreasing in arithmetical progression. Hence the buffalo hunting/hunted lore sharpens only our hind-claws rather than you know what – unless we go metric.

It is not difficult to distinguish these country rats. Most of them are found inhabiting the bushes on the sunset side of the core, or are found in sandland up straight where they are blocking the blood-flow south. But, of course like adventitious plants, country rats are found everywhere, even unrooted.

Two more tasks and our abstract is over. Let's dispose with the moths first. These come out at night, rush straight to any light where they are lucky if only their wings are singed. Why they always rush headlong to their deaths like bulls I don't know. But, just as a fool cannot die a martyr's death, so nobody should waste tears over one more moth suicidal. Let's then conclude with Mr. Town Rat. Is he a fish out of water? Or has water flowed uphill leaving him exposed? (We fully believe that steam, air, clouds, and ice are forms of water. Hence water can climb hills and Kilimanjaros like Noah's boat if the mountains cannot come to Mohammed.) Now, due to a drastic decrease in infant mortality and the increase of sanitation, ease of contact, the possession of larger ears making them most excitable to other reverberations from other parts of the cactus, Town-rats are in great increase.

But, when they talk among us and speak of cat-traps, is this ancheomemory, a tongue-twister, a fondling of the navel where our umbilicold was, or what? Nabat akhen-a-Ghose made frequent allusions to this loseable art.

One thing is clear: town-rats talk of fire-sticks, bush-reducation, and rat (in general) life, if not survival and increase in a more virile form.

Chapter(s) to be written on the unknown Batsiary(ies) that will come to light.) But trespassers should never be prosecuted, or which is worse, persecuted. No need to worry. Sanigraland batsiaries are also an elusive lot. They can promote themselves into gentlemen; but we, with pain, can reduce them into hearts, heads, noise, cough-mixtures.